THE TIGER: APEX PREDATOR OF THE JUNGLE

Big Cats: Nature's Perfection
Series

Book 1\7

By Rayan Cutler

Table of Contents

Introduction

The tiger, with its powerful frame, mesmerizing coat of orange and black, and piercing gaze, stands as one of nature's most formidable predators. As the largest of the big cats, the tiger commands respect not only for its physical strength but also for its cunning and adaptability. Across Asia, tigers have long been a symbol of power, courage, and beauty, captivating people in cultures and traditions that date back centuries. From the moment you encounter this majestic creature, it's clear that the tiger is an apex predator — a true ruler of its domain.

The tiger's reign stretches across some of the most diverse habitats in the world. From the dense jungles of India to the remote forests of Siberia, tigers have evolved to survive and thrive in environments that can be as harsh as they are beautiful. The tiger's extraordinary abilities — strength, stealth, and speed — allow it to dominate its territory, hunting with precision and grace. With jaws that deliver one of the most powerful bite forces among land mammals, a muscular build designed for sprinting, and keen instincts, the tiger is perfectly equipped for its role at the top of the food chain.

But the tiger's story is not only one of strength and survival. It is also a tale of vulnerability. Despite its dominance in the wild, the tiger faces a number of challenges in the modern world. Habitat loss, poaching, and human-wildlife conflict have led to a decline in tiger populations. In this book, we will explore how conservation efforts are working to protect these magnificent creatures and ensure their survival for future generations.

This book is the first in a series that will explore the most powerful and iconic big cats of the world. In this series, we will take an in-depth look at each species — from the tiger to the lion, jaguar, leopard, cheetah, puma, and snow leopard. Each book in this series will offer insight into what makes these big cats so unique, their vital role in the ecosystem, and the challenges they face in a rapidly changing world.

As we delve into the life of the tiger in this first book, we will examine its anatomy, strength, speed, and the hunting techniques that make it an unrivaled predator. From the dense jungles where it roams to its solitary nature, we will uncover the secrets of the tiger's existence and how it continues to thrive despite the many obstacles it faces. We will also explore the dangers that threaten its existence, tracing how close the tiger has come—and still is—to extinction. Furthermore, we'll examine its presence in art, cultures, poems, and tales, uncovering how humans have viewed and celebrated this majestic animal throughout history. All of this and more will be explained in this book, offering a comprehensive understanding of one of the most fascinating animals on Earth.

CHAPTER I:

THE ORIGINS OF A PREDATOR

The story of the tiger, one of the most revered predators on Earth, begins not just with its own lineage but with the broader history of the cat family. As the first book in this series, it's fitting to explore the origins of the Felidae family—the evolutionary group that connects all cats, from the diminutive domestic feline to the formidable tiger. This chapter will chart the tiger's journey through deep time, tracing its evolutionary roots, the emergence of the Panthera genus, and its place within the wider world of large cats, including those that don't strictly qualify as "big cats" by scientific standards but have earned their place in this series due to their stature and significance.

The Dawn of Feliformia: The Early Ancestors:

The evolutionary journey of tigers begins around 40-50 million years ago, during the Eocene epoch. At this time, Earth's landscapes were dominated by dense forests and a warm climate, which fostered the rise of early carnivorous mammals. Among these was a group known as Carnivoraformes, the ancestors of modern carnivores. Within this group, a distinct lineage known as Feliformia emerged, characterized by their sharp teeth, agility, and predatory instincts.

These early feliforms were small, tree-dwelling predators that relied on stealth and quick strikes to hunt. Over millions of years, they diversified into various forms, evolving adaptations like retractable claws and acute vision—traits that would become hallmarks of the modern cat family.

The Rise of the Felidae Family:

Fast forward to around 25-30 million years ago, and the Felidae family—the true cats—came into existence. These early cats were highly specialized hunters, with bodies designed for speed, precision, and power. Fossil evidence suggests they first appeared in Asia, from where they spread to other continents.

The Felidae family eventually split into two main subfamilies:

- **Pantherinae:** The roaring big cats, such as lions, tigers, leopards, and jaguars.
- **Felinae:** Smaller cats, including domestic cats, cheetahs, and pumas.

This division set the stage for the evolution of the tiger and its close relatives, as well as the development of unique adaptations in each group.

The Panthera Genus: Masters of the Wild:

Within the Pantherinae subfamily, the Panthera genus began to emerge approximately 2-3 million years ago. Members of this group are distinguished by their ability to roar, thanks to a specialized larynx and a flexible hyoid bone. This genus includes the tiger, lion, leopard, and jaguar—all iconic big cats that dominate their respective environments.

Among the Panthera cats, the tiger evolved into the largest and most solitary predator. Fossil evidence indicates that early tigers roamed the forests and grasslands of Asia, adapting to a wide range of habitats. Their distinct orange coat with black stripes evolved as camouflage, enabling them to ambush prey with unparalleled precision.

Clarifying the "Big Cat" Category:

It's important to address a common misconception about big cats. Scientifically, the term "big cat" refers specifically to members of the Panthera genus—lions, tigers, leopards, and jaguars—because they share the unique ability to roar. However, other large felines, such as cheetahs and pumas, are often included in this category due to their size, strength, and role as apex predators.

Cheetahs, for example, belong to the Felinae subfamily and lack the physical structure to roar, yet their incredible speed and hunting prowess have made them one of the most recognizable big cats in popular culture. Similarly, the puma, also a Felinae member, is not a true big cat but is often grouped with them because of its impressive size and adaptability.

In this series, we include cheetahs and pumas as honorary big cats, recognizing their importance and the fascination they inspire, despite their technical classification.

The Evolutionary Path of Tigers:

The tiger's ancestors likely diverged from other Panthera species around 2 million years ago. Early tigers were highly adaptable, thriving in diverse environments ranging from the frozen landscapes of Siberia to the tropical forests of Southeast Asia. Over time, they developed unique features such as elongated limbs for stealthy movement, powerful jaws capable of crushing bone, and their iconic stripes, which provide exceptional camouflage in dappled light.

Fossil records from regions like China and Indonesia reveal that these proto-tigers were already formidable predators, capable of hunting large herbivores and competing with other carnivores for dominance. Their adaptability allowed them to survive climatic changes and expand their range, becoming one of the most widespread big cats in history.

Tigers and Their Place in the Natural World:
As the largest member of the Panthera genus, the tiger represents the pinnacle of feline evolution. Its journey from a small, tree-dwelling ancestor to the apex predator we admire today is a testament to the resilience and adaptability of the Felidae family.

One of the most remarkable aspects of the tiger's evolution is how it carved out a unique niche as the ultimate solitary predator. Unlike lions, which rely on pride dynamics for hunting and protection, tigers developed an independent strategy for survival. This divergence likely occurred due to environmental factors, such as denser forest habitats that favored solitary hunting over group cooperation. Tigers honed their stealth and ambush tactics to perfection, using their powerful limbs and sharp claws to take down prey several times their size. This specialization is reflected in their anatomy: a large cranial capacity for acute senses, muscular builds optimized for short bursts of power, and, of course, their iconic stripes that enhance their ability to blend seamlessly into their surroundings. These evolutionary traits not only ensured their dominance in the wild but also set them apart from other big cats as masters of solitary predation.

Humans and Tigers: Ancient Fears and Fascinations:

The first recorded interactions between humans and tigers likely date back tens of thousands of years, as early humans began to share habitats with these formidable predators. Evidence from ancient cave paintings, such as those found in the Indonesian island of Sulawesi, suggests that early humans not only feared but also revered tigers. These large cats were both a threat and a symbol of power. In the dense jungles and grasslands of Asia, tigers may have been one of the earliest apex predators that humans encountered regularly, forcing them to develop strategies for survival.

 As humans transitioned from nomadic to settled lifestyles, their relationship with tigers grew more complex. Tigers often prowled near villages, attracted by livestock or weaker prey, leading to both conflict and mythology. In some early Asian cultures, tigers became symbols of strength and protection, while in others, they represented untamed danger. Archeological evidence, such as tiger remains found near ancient human settlements in India and China, suggests that humans hunted tigers for their pelts and bones, perhaps even for spiritual rituals. Meanwhile, legends of tigers stalking hunters in return emerged, further embedding the animal in the cultural psyche as a creature to be both feared and respected.

 This dynamic interplay between human ingenuity and the tiger's unmatched power underscores how deeply intertwined their histories are. These early encounters not only shaped human survival tactics but also influenced the cultural significance of tigers, setting the stage for their iconic status in art, folklore, and even religion.

This chapter sets the stage for the rest of the book, where we will delve into the tiger's anatomy, behavior, and role in ecosystems. From their origins to their current challenges, tigers embody both the beauty and the fragility of the natural world. By understanding their past, we can better appreciate their present and work toward ensuring their future.

CHAPTER 2:
STRIPES IN THE WILD: HABITATS AND DISTRIBUTION

As many of you may not know, there is more than one tiger subspecies. While most people are familiar with the Siberian tiger, renowned for its massive size and snowy habitat, and the Bengal tiger, the iconic predator of India's forests, these are just two representatives of a family of 6 subspecies. Tigers are among nature's most awe-inspiring creatures, their majestic forms seamlessly blending power and elegance. Each tiger subspecies is a testament to the adaptability and resilience of life, thriving in environments as diverse as the icy forests of Siberia, the humid mangroves of the Sundarbans, and the dense rainforests of Sumatra. This incredible diversity highlights their unparalleled strength and mastery over their respective domains. Every tiger, in its unique habitat, reigns supreme, showcasing the remarkable capacity of evolution to shape these apex predators into rulers of their surroundings.

Bengal Tiger: Lord of the Grasslands and Mangroves:

The Bengal tiger, scientifically known as Panthera tigris tigris, is one of the most iconic and powerful predators of the wild, commanding respect across its expansive territories. Found primarily in the vast and diverse landscapes of India, Bangladesh, Nepal, Bhutan, and Myanmar, the Bengal tiger reigns supreme in the grasslands, mangroves, and dense forests. What makes the Bengal tiger so uniquely formidable is not just its imposing size or strength, but its adaptability to various habitats. From the hot, humid swamps of the Sundarbans mangrove forests, where it navigates the tidal waterways with stealth, to the dry, scrubby grasslands that stretch across northern India, this tiger thrives in environments as diverse as the prey it hunts.

One of the Bengal tiger's most remarkable traits is its ability to adapt to these different landscapes. In the thick, waterlogged terrain of the Sundarbans, for example, the tiger's muscular limbs and webbed paws allow it to swim effortlessly, making it a dominant force in the mangrove ecosystem. This unique adaptation gives the Bengal tiger an edge, as it can hunt both on land and in water, targeting prey such as wild boars, deer, and even the occasional saltwater crocodile. Meanwhile, in the dry, open grasslands of the Terai region, its golden, striped coat helps it blend into the tall grasses, waiting patiently for the right moment to pounce. The Bengal tiger is an apex predator, a perfect example of how evolution has equipped it to thrive in multiple environments, from coastal marshlands to dense tropical forests.

Historically, the Bengal tiger once roamed over much larger areas, but today, its habitat is significantly reduced. As human populations have expanded, many of the tiger's natural homes have been encroached upon, reducing their numbers and forcing these magnificent creatures into increasingly fragmented regions. Despite this, Bengal tigers remain one of the most populous tiger subspecies, though their numbers are still critically threatened due to habitat loss, poaching, and human-wildlife conflict. The situation remains dire, but conservation efforts in India, such as the Project Tiger initiative, have seen some success in creating protected areas and wildlife reserves that offer a safer environment for these big cats. The fight to preserve the Bengal tiger continues, and it serves as a symbol not only of the majesty of the wild but also of the importance of safeguarding the ecosystems on which it depends.

The Siberian Tiger: Guardians of the Frozen Taiga:

The Siberian tiger, a majestic creature of the frozen wilderness, is a living testament to resilience. Also known as the Amur tiger, it roams the harsh, snow-covered landscapes of the Russian Far East, inhabiting the dense Taiga forests and rugged mountain regions. The environment it calls home is like no other—long, bitterly cold winters and short, mild summers, creating a challenging yet perfect setting for this incredible predator. The Siberian tiger is not only built to survive in these extreme conditions but to thrive. With a thick, dense coat of fur that insulates it from freezing temperatures and wide paws that act like snowshoes, the Siberian tiger has evolved to dominate its icy kingdom. Its coat, which turns from a bright orange in the summer to a deeper, more muted shade during the winter months, blends seamlessly with the snowy backdrop, allowing it to hunt stealthily.

This tiger is a solitary and silent guardian of its frozen realm, rarely seen and even less frequently understood. The Taiga, with its towering pines and sprawling snowfields, is a land of both beauty and danger, where survival is a constant struggle against the bitter cold, the lack of prey in some areas, and encroaching human activity. However, the Siberian tiger is nothing short of a marvel in its ability to endure. Even amidst all of this, it remains the top predator in its region. It can take down prey as large as moose and wild boar, using its incredible strength and skill to subdue even the toughest opponents. Its territory, stretching over hundreds of square miles, is a fortress that this solitary hunter fiercely defends, ensuring it remains the ruler of its frigid domain.

The Siberian tiger's habitat is nothing short of breathtaking, yet merciless. The Taiga, a vast expanse of evergreen forests, dense underbrush, and frozen rivers, forms the perfect backdrop for this cold-weather monarch. Temperatures in this region can plummet to as low as -40°F (-40°C) during the winter months, making it one of the coldest places on Earth for a tiger to call home. But the Siberian tiger thrives in these extreme conditions, its thick fur coat and layer of fat providing it with the insulation needed to survive such freezing temperatures. In the brief summer months, the Taiga turns into a lush, green landscape of tall grasses and dense forests. These forests are often shrouded in mist, with towering trees that create a canopy high above, offering the tiger ample cover to stalk its prey silently. The combination of cold, isolated snowfields and dense woodland makes the Siberian tiger an undisputed ruler of its environment, where every aspect of its anatomy has been tailored to adapt to and dominate this tough landscape. Whether it's silently padding across the snow or darting between trees, the Siberian tiger remains an enigmatic presence in the untouched wilderness of the Russian Far East, a perfect embodiment of the harsh beauty and isolation of its home.

The Sumatran Tiger: Hidden Shadows of the Rainforest:

The Sumatran tiger, the smallest and most elusive of the tiger subspecies, is a master of disguise, blending seamlessly into the lush, dense rainforests of Indonesia's Sumatran islands. This tiger's environment is a world of perpetual twilight, where sunlight barely pierces the dense canopy of towering tropical trees. The jungle floor, carpeted in a mosaic of fallen leaves, vines, and moss-covered roots, provides a labyrinth of hiding spots for the Sumatran tiger. Its striped coat—narrower and darker than that of its larger relatives—acts as the ultimate camouflage, mimicking the dappled shadows of its forest home.

Living in such a diverse and densely packed ecosystem, the Sumatran tiger has adapted to a variety of prey, from wild boars and deer to smaller mammals like monkeys. The tiger's small frame and powerful agility give it an edge in navigating the thick undergrowth and climbing when necessary—a rare skill among tigers. Here, every step is a calculated movement, every hunt a silent game of patience, as prey often remains just out of reach in the trees or under cover of dense foliage.

The rainforest itself breathes life into this tiger, with its humid air, flowing rivers, and occasional waterfalls creating a symphony of sound that the tiger uses to mask its movements. The island's mangroves and peat swamps are no less important, as they offer unique hunting grounds and serve as vital corridors for the tiger to roam. These rainforests, rich in biodiversity, are the perfect stage for the Sumatran tiger's quiet reign— a world where it rules from the shadows, a living embodiment of mystery and grace.

The Indochinese Tiger: Hunters of Southeast Asia:

The Indochinese tiger, a cunning and powerful predator, roams the rugged mountains, dense forests, and river valleys of Southeast Asia with unmatched stealth and precision. Found in countries like Vietnam, Thailand, Laos, Cambodia, and Myanmar, this subspecies is perfectly adapted to thrive in some of the most challenging terrains on Earth. Their coats are darker and more muted in color than their Bengal relatives, with narrower stripes that help them blend seamlessly into the dappled shadows of their surroundings. Every inch of their habitat—whether it be the humid jungles or the rocky hillsides—is a playground for this adaptable hunter.

Indochinese tigers are opportunistic feeders, preying on a variety of animals, from wild pigs and deer to smaller creatures like porcupines and birds. Their patience and sharp instincts make them masters of ambush, often lying in wait near water sources where prey gathers. What makes them particularly remarkable is their resilience in environments where prey is often scarce and competition fierce. They embody the spirit of survival, using their keen senses and unparalleled agility to carve out a niche in a world of constant danger and scarcity.

These tigers are not just hunters but symbols of the intricate and fragile ecosystems they inhabit. Their territories often overlap with those of elephants, leopards, and countless other species, creating a delicate balance that showcases the interconnectedness of life in Southeast Asia. Unfortunately, the region's rapid deforestation and human encroachment are pushing these majestic creatures further into isolation. Yet, in the wild depths of Indochina, the tiger's roar still echoes—a haunting reminder of its enduring legacy and a call to protect the lands it has ruled for ages.

Malayan Tigers: Hiding Gems of Malaysia:

Deep within the tropical rainforests of the Malay Peninsula, an elusive jewel prowls— the Malayan tiger (Panthera tigris jacksoni). These compact yet powerful predators are renowned for their adaptability and their enigmatic presence. They thrive in one of the most biodiverse ecosystems on Earth, where humid jungles are laced with dense foliage and rolling hills. Despite their relatively smaller size compared to their Siberian and Bengal cousins, Malayan tigers are masters of stealth and agility, perfectly suited to their labyrinthine habitat of thick forests and swamps.

The Malayan tiger, officially recognized as a distinct subspecies only in 2004, has a unique heritage and identity. Sharing its home with creatures like tapirs, sun bears, and elephants, this tiger has evolved to be a consummate predator in a lush but challenging environment. Their territories often span through lowlands and montane forests, requiring them to navigate rugged terrain and unpredictable climates. Malayan tigers are known to ambush prey with lightning precision, relying on their camouflaged coats to blend seamlessly into their surroundings.

While they exude an aura of dominance, their story is tinged with vulnerability. These tigers are symbols of pride in Malaysia, even adorning the nation's coat of arms. But the forests they call home are shrinking, forcing these "hiding gems" into increasingly smaller pockets of wilderness. For centuries, they have ruled their realm, an unyielding testament to the raw beauty and resilience of nature in Southeast Asia.

South China Tigers: Ghosts of the Wild:

Rarely seen and shrouded in mystery, the South China tiger is more myth than reality in the modern wilderness. Known as the "ghosts of the wild," these tigers once roamed vast stretches of southern China's subtropical forests and mountains. Adapted to a landscape of steep ridges, dense bamboo thickets, and evergreen forests, the South China tiger was a symbol of strength and resilience in an ancient and rugged terrain.

Unlike its more famous relatives, this tiger evolved to thrive in warmer, less predictable climates, where summers can be sweltering and winters chilly but not extreme. These predators are slightly smaller than Bengal tigers, with shorter fur and brighter, more vibrant orange coats—an aesthetic masterpiece of natural camouflage against the forest undergrowth. They were once apex predators in their domain, balancing ecosystems by preying on ungulates like deer and wild boar.

But the South China tiger's realm is now a shadow of its former glory. Centuries of deforestation, human expansion, and hunting have turned their vast territory into fragmented patches of wilderness. While their historic range spanned provinces like Guangdong, Fujian, and Jiangxi, their habitat today is more memory than reality. Conservation efforts have sparked a glimmer of hope, as breeding programs in captivity aim to reintroduce them to the wild.

Though the South China tiger is considered functionally extinct in the wild, it is not fully extinct. A small population survives in carefully managed reserves, representing a critical opportunity for preservation. These living ghosts remind us of nature's fragility and humanity's responsibility to protect what remains of our shared world.

It is truly awe-inspiring how each tiger has mastered its unique environment, adapting to climates and terrains as diverse as the frozen taigas of Siberia, the dense rainforests of Sumatra, and the sunlit grasslands of India. Each tiger's stripes are not just patterns but symbols of evolution's artistry, designed to dominate and blend within their respective realms. From the biting cold to searing heat, these apex predators have evolved to rule their territories with unparalleled strength and skill. Their diversity is a testament to nature's ingenuity, showcasing how life thrives against all odds in vastly different conditions. This majestic adaptability is what cements the tiger's place as one of the most extraordinary creatures to ever walk the earth.

CHAPTER 3:
THE MEASURE OF POWER

The physical majesty of tigers is a study in awe-inspiring adaptation. From their immense size to their dense bones and rippling musculature, tigers are perfectly sculpted for dominance. Though measuring them can be tricky due to variations within populations and individual specimens, the Siberian and Bengal tigers stand out as the heaviest and longest subspecies, while the other four display their unique adaptations to diverse habitats.

The Siberian Titan:

The Siberian tiger (Panthera tigris altaica) is the largest of all tigers, often considered nature's masterpiece of raw power and endurance. Males typically weigh 397 to 650 pounds (180–295 kg), with exceptional individuals reaching up to 700 pounds (318 kg). Their overall length, including the tail, spans an impressive 9.5 to 12 feet (290–365 cm). Females, though smaller, remain formidable predators, weighing 220 to 370 pounds (100–170 kg) and measuring 8.5 to 10 feet (260–310 cm).

A Siberian tiger's physical prowess isn't limited to its size; its dense bones and heavily muscled frame provide it with unmatched strength and durability. The added bulk isn't a burden in their snowy habitat but an asset, enabling them to overpower large prey and endure long, harsh winters.

The Bengal Powerhouse:
Equally captivating is the Bengal tiger (Panthera tigris tigris), an apex predator of the lush landscapes of India and its neighboring countries. Male Bengals average 397 to 569 pounds (180–258 kg) and reach lengths of 9 to 10.8 feet (275–330 cm), including the tail. Some exceptional specimens have tipped the scales at over 600 pounds (272 kg). Females, though lighter, weigh between 220 to 350 pounds (100–160 kg) and measure 8 to 9.5 feet (245–290 cm).

The Bengal tiger mirrors the Siberian in strength and athleticism, boasting equally dense bones and a powerful physique. Their adaptations allow them to hunt anything from swift deer to massive gaur, making them supreme rulers of their tropical and subtropical territories.

The Quartet of Adaptability:
The other four subspecies—the Indochinese tiger, Malayan tiger, South China tiger, and Sumatran tiger—embody versatility and evolution. Males range in size from 220 to 440 pounds (100–200 kg)

and measure 8 to 10 feet (250–310 cm), while females weigh 165 to 265 pounds (75–120 kg) and measure 7.5 to 8.5 feet (230–260 cm).

The Sumatran tiger, the smallest of them all, is a compact marvel, with males rarely exceeding 310 pounds (140 kg). Despite their size, their dense musculature ensures they remain apex predators in the dense jungles of Sumatra. Meanwhile, the South China tiger, on the brink of extinction, serves as a poignant reminder of the importance of conservation efforts.

Siberian vs. Bengal: A Hypothetical Duel:

If a clash between a Siberian tiger and a Bengal tiger were to occur, the result would be as close as their physical measurements. The differences between these two giants often come down to just 22 to 110 pounds (10–50 kg), making it difficult to declare a definitive winner. Both possess similar speed, agility, and predatory instincts, but the Siberian tiger's slight advantage in size and bulk gives it a narrow edge.

Ultimately, the outcome could go either way, as much depends on the individuals involved. However, if one had to pick, the Siberian tiger's extra size and resilience make it the likeliest victor. In the next book, focused on lions, we will explore the classic debate of whether a tiger, particularly a Siberian, could outmatch the lion in a battle for supremacy.

Please note that determining the exact weight of these majestic beasts can be somewhat challenging due to the natural variability in size and weight across individuals, influenced by factors such as diet, environment, and genetics. Additionally, precise measurements can be difficult to obtain in the wild or even in captivity, where conditions may vary significantly. What is essential to understand is that the Siberian tiger, also known as the Amur tiger, is slightly larger on average than other tiger subspecies, such as the Bengal tiger. This size difference is generally attributed to its adaptations to the colder climates of its habitat, requiring more substantial body mass for insulation and energy reserves. While specific numbers may fluctuate, the overarching takeaway remains: the Siberian tiger stands as the largest of all tiger subspecies, a true testament to the grandeur of these apex predators.

It is a common misconception that the Siberian

tiger has shrunk in size due to the loss of habitat and prey. This idea, while widespread, is not supported by scientific evidence. The primary impact of habitat loss and a decline in prey availability has been a significant reduction in the tiger's population, not a change in its physical size or body mass. Such a transformation in average body size would likely require thousands of years of evolutionary pressure to occur, and there has been no such time frame or evidence for this within the context of the Siberian tiger's recent history. This misunderstanding may stem from comparing individual tigers of different subspecies or environmental conditions. For instance, Bengal tigers in captivity are often well-fed, sometimes excessively so, and can even become obese if overfed and under-exercised. Comparing these captive Bengal tigers to wild Siberian tigers, which naturally maintain leaner physiques due to their active and demanding lifestyles, is misleading. Captivity significantly alters a tiger's physical condition, making such comparisons unreliable. It is crucial to base observations on proper scientific data and avoid conflating the challenges of habitat loss with unsubstantiated claims about physical shrinkage.

CHAPTER 4: THE PREDATOR'S ARSENAL

The Siberian tiger is a creature built for dominance, equipped with an extraordinary set of weapons that make it one of the most efficient predators in the animal kingdom. Its vast array of lethal tools, including powerful jaws, sharp claws, and impressive muscle mass, enable it to rule its environment. While the Bengal tiger shares many of these same traits, the Siberian tiger's size and strength make it particularly formidable in the wild.

One of the most defining features of the Siberian tiger is its bite force, a critical asset in subduing prey. With a bite force of around 1,050 PSI, the Siberian tiger has the ability to crush bone and sever the windpipe of large prey with a single, deadly strike. The Bengal tiger, while slightly smaller, shares a comparable bite force, capable of inflicting similar damage. Both tigers have upper canines that can grow up to 3.5 inches (9 cm) in length, allowing them to pierce deep into flesh. These teeth are vital for gripping and holding onto their prey, particularly when dealing with large, struggling animals. This bite force is one of the tiger's most lethal weapons, making it an apex predator.

In addition to their powerful jaws, both tigers boast

retractable claws that can grow up to 4 inches (10 cm). These claws are designed for more than just climbing trees; they serve as deadly tools during hunts, allowing the tiger to grab onto prey with unmatched precision and force. Whether it is tearing through skin or immobilizing a struggling animal, these claws are invaluable tools in the tiger's arsenal. The Siberian tiger, with its larger paws, uses its claws effectively in snowy conditions, while the Bengal tiger's claws are equally adept in its dense jungle habitat.

But a tiger's power isn't limited to its bite and claws alone. Their muscular build and bone density further enhance their predatory capabilities. A Siberian tiger's strength lies in its powerful shoulders and forelimbs, allowing it to overpower and drag prey that is often much larger than itself. Their bodies are designed to efficiently deliver short bursts of speed, especially during an ambush, and their forelimbs are strong enough to tackle large, heavy prey such as elk or moose. The tiger's bones are dense and durable, designed to withstand the impact of powerful blows during a hunt. This makes them incredibly resilient, ensuring they can deliver a fatal blow to their prey, even when it is a formidable adversary.

Speaking of speed, the Siberian tiger is not just a powerhouse but also surprisingly fast. It can reach speeds of up to 37 miles per hour (60 km/h) for short bursts, an impressive feat for an animal of its size. The Bengal tiger, too, is fast, capable of reaching 40 miles per hour (64 km/h) in its prime. However, speed is not the defining trait of these big cats; their raw strength and ambush tactics often render speed less important. Tigers do not rely on chasing prey across long distances but instead use stealth to get as close as possible before launching a quick, explosive charge.

Both the Siberian and Bengal tigers are stealth hunters, moving silently through their habitats, whether in the dense jungles of India or the snow-covered forests of Russia. Their ability to remain undetected while stalking prey is enhanced by their exceptional camouflage, with the Siberian tiger's thick, pale fur blending perfectly into snowy environments, and the Bengal tiger's orange-and-black stripes allowing it to melt into the underbrush of its tropical forests.

While both tigers are formidable predators with similar weaponry and hunting strategies, the Siberian tiger stands out in terms of sheer size and power. Its larger size means it has the muscle mass to tackle even heavier prey, often overpowering animals that might be too difficult for the Bengal tiger. Whether it is a large elk, a wild boar, or even a bear, the Siberian tiger's physical advantage gives it an edge in taking down prey that requires raw power rather than agility.

Both tigers are exceptional in their respective environments, each perfectly adapted to their surroundings. The Siberian tiger's arsenal of weapons, combined with its greater size and strength, make it a dominant force in the wild, capable of handling larger and more challenging prey. The Bengal tiger, while slightly smaller, is equally equipped with the same deadly tools, making it no less a fearsome predator in its own right. The difference lies in their environments, with the Siberian tiger's physical attributes lending themselves well to the harsh, cold terrain of the Russian Far East, while the Bengal tiger's agility is well-suited to its dense jungle habitat.

The tiger's arsenal of impressive physical attributes, including its powerful bite force, sharp retractable claws, and immense muscular build, make it one of the deadliest animals on Earth. With the ability to subdue prey much larger than itself, these weapons not only ensure its dominance in the wild but also cement its status as an apex predator. Its sheer strength, agility, and natural hunting tactics combine to create a creature perfectly evolved to thrive in the harshest environments, making it a true marvel of nature's design.

CHAPTER 5:
TIGERS AND THEIR PREY

Tigers are equipped with some of the most impressive physical attributes in the animal kingdom, and their bite force is one of the most awe-inspiring. A tiger's bite force can exceed 1,000 psi (pounds per square inch). To put that in perspective, a human bite force averages around 160 psi—just a fraction of the tiger's incredible strength. This immense force enables tigers to puncture through thick hides, crush bones, and dispatch prey with precision. The tiger's powerful bite, along with its retractable claws and muscular build, makes it a deadly predator. This bite is crucial for bringing down large prey like deer and wild boar, and in some rare cases, even bears, with the weight of these animals ranging from 100 kilograms (220 pounds) to over 1,000 kilograms (2,200 pounds) in some cases.. The sheer force of a tiger's bite is more than enough to sever an artery or break the neck of an animal in a single strike.

Despite the variety of prey available to tigers, their success rate in hunting remains relatively low. Tigers typically only succeed in around 10 to 20% of their hunts, a reflection of the difficulty in catching large, fast, and alert prey. However, this low success rate does not diminish their reputation as efficient hunters. When they do strike, they do so with impressive power and precision. Tigers do not rely on stamina or long chases to capture their prey, as their bodies are not built for endurance running. Unlike wolves, which hunt in packs and chase prey over long distances, tigers are built for short bursts of speed. Their muscles are designed for powerful sprints, and they can reach speeds of up to 60 kilometers per hour (37 miles per hour) in short bursts. However, this burst of speed is typically reserved for the final pounce, when the tiger has already stalked its prey close enough to make a surprise attack. This strategy allows them to conserve energy, which is crucial given the low success rate of their hunts.

While a tiger's striking colors—its orange coat and black stripes—are easily visible to humans and other predators in the wild, it's worth noting that many animals, particularly prey species, cannot see these colors as we do. Tigers are typically colorblind to red and green, so their bright orange fur blends much more effectively with their surroundings when viewed by their prey, especially in the twilight or dense forest environments where tigers often hunt. The camouflage provided by their stripes helps them to remain concealed from the watchful eyes of herbivores, which rely on sight to detect predators. Most herbivores, including deer and wild boar, have a limited ability to detect the tiger's true form against the backdrop of the environment. For these prey, tigers are often invisible until they are within striking distance.

While their ability to hunt is impressive, tigers are solitary animals, unlike pack hunters such as wolves. They rely on their stealth and camouflage, aided by their striped fur, to approach their prey as quietly as possible. The element of surprise is essential for a successful hunt. Once within range, a tiger will use its powerful legs to launch a rapid, explosive charge toward the prey, often closing the distance in seconds.

When it comes to bears, it is true that tigers are capable of attacking and even killing brown bears, but this is often misunderstood as a common behavior. Tigers, with their immense strength and powerful hunting techniques, do not typically prey on healthy adult bears. In most instances where a tiger successfully kills a bear, it is usually a younger, smaller, or weaker bear, such as one that is sick, old, or undernourished. Additionally, tigers may take advantage of a bear that is temporarily vulnerable, such as when it is hibernating or asleep during the winter months. This rare interaction showcases the tiger's ability to take on large and formidable prey, but it is not a frequent or regular part of their diet. Generally, tigers prefer to hunt more manageable prey, like deer or wild boar, as these are less risky targets compared to the mighty brown bear.

If a healthy male brown bear were to fight a healthy male tiger, the battle's outcome would heavily depend on the specific circumstances and individuals involved. While pound for pound, a tiger might have an advantage due to its speed, agility, and bite force, the sheer size of a large male brown bear would give it a substantial edge. Brown bears can weigh up to 1,500 pounds (680 kilograms) or more, which is 2 times the typical size of a large male tiger. The size difference alone would make it extremely difficult for the tiger to overcome the bear, as bears are built to fight with strong, powerful forelimbs and massive claws.

Bears are not only larger but are also specifically evolved for survival and combat. They are often engaged in physical battles for territory or mating rights, and their physical structure is adapted to handle such confrontations. On the other hand, tigers are solitary hunters, and while their powerful bite and agility are formidable, they are not generally built to take on creatures as large as a healthy male bear.

The idea of a tiger and a bear fighting is more of an internet debate rather than a natural scenario. Tigers would not typically encounter bears in the wild in this context, as there is no territorial or mate-related conflict between the two species. In the wild, tigers tend to avoid confrontations with animals larger than themselves unless necessary. Therefore, it's important to note that while this matchup might be entertaining to speculate about, it is highly unlikely to happen in the wild. A tiger would not typically engage a male bear unless forced to by circumstance, and a healthy, large male brown bear would have a significant advantage in such a situation.

Despite their impressive hunting skills, tigers are not invincible. They face numerous challenges in the wild, including avoiding injury during a failed hunt or when dealing with large, dangerous prey. Even though they have a powerful bite and great strength, tigers do not always succeed. Their ability to adapt and learn from each failure is key to their survival, ensuring that when they do succeed, they do so with deadly efficiency.

CHAPTER 6:

A DAY IN THE LIFE OF A TIGER

This chapter takes you deep into the daily life of a tiger, blending reality with imagination to craft an intimate and vivid tale. The protagonist is a colossal Siberian tiger, a 650-pound male, roaming the snow-covered wilderness of the Russian Far East. Through this narrative, you'll experience his struggles, triumphs, and the intricate details of his existence. Each fact woven into the story is rooted in the reality of a tiger's life, allowing you to walk beside him in his world.

The first rays of the sun filter through the dense canopy of the boreal forest, casting long shadows over a land blanketed in frost and snow. The tiger stirs in his den, a hollow beneath the sprawling roots of an ancient pine. His immense body, over 11 feet long from nose to tail, shifts as he stretches, claws extending to rake the frozen earth. Steam rises from his breath as it meets the crisp, biting air, and his amber eyes glint with the fire of life. Hunger gnaws at him—a familiar companion—and today he must eat.

He steps into the forest, each movement deliberate and silent. The sheer size of this tiger is awe-inspiring, his muscles rippling beneath a thick coat of fur that insulates him from temperatures plunging to -40°F. At 650 pounds, he is one of nature's most formidable predators, yet the challenge of survival never wanes. He pauses to scent the air, his powerful olfactory senses detecting the faint musk of a herd of deer several miles away. With a low rumble, more felt than heard, he begins his journey.

The tiger navigates the forest with remarkable ease, his stripes blending into the interplay of light and shadow. While his vivid coloration seems stark to the human eye, to his prey—many of whom perceive the world in shades of gray—he is nearly invisible. This natural camouflage is one of the many evolutionary advantages that make him a master of the hunt.

Hours pass as he tracks the deer, his patience as formidable as his strength. Eventually, he spots his quarry: a large red deer grazing in a snow-dappled clearing. This prey, weighing close to 500 pounds, represents a substantial meal. The tiger crouches low, his body a coiled spring of muscle and intent. Slowly, methodically, he edges closer, every step silent on the snow-covered ground.

When the moment is right, he explodes into action, covering over 30 feet in a single bound. His acceleration is astonishing, reaching speeds of up to 40 miles per hour, though only for a brief burst. The deer bolts, but the tiger's claws sink into its flank, dragging it to the ground. The final blow comes with his powerful jaws, capable of exerting over 1,000 pounds per square inch of pressure—ten times the strength of a human bite. This force is enough to crush the deer's windpipe, ensuring a swift and merciful kill.

The tiger begins his feast, tearing into the flesh with ease. In one sitting, he can consume up to 90 pounds of meat, a necessity for sustaining his immense body. This meal will fuel him for days, though he must guard it fiercely from scavengers like wolves and bears. Despite his dominance, survival in the wild is a constant battle, and even the king of the forest must remain vigilant.

As the day progresses, the tiger engages in other essential activities. He patrols his vast territory, covering over 200 square miles, and marks his domain by scratching trees and spraying scent. These signs warn rivals of his presence, reducing the likelihood of direct confrontations. The tiger also sharpens his claws on the bark of trees, maintaining the lethal weapons that are crucial to his survival.

 Twilight descends, painting the forest in hues of gold and blue. The tiger finds a quiet spot near a frozen stream and drinks deeply, his rough tongue lapping at the icy water. He rests briefly, his ears swiveling at every sound, ever alert to the dangers of the wilderness. As night falls, the temperature plummets, but his thick fur and immense body keep him warm.

 Returning to his den, the tiger lies down, his belly full and his spirit content. The wilderness hums softly around him, a symphony of life and survival. As he closes his eyes, the forest becomes still, and the cycle of his existence begins anew.

 And just as the tiger begins to drift into a deep slumber, the faint sound of howling pierces the stillness of the forest. His ears twitch, then his amber eyes snap open, glowing faintly in the moonlight. The sound is close, too close. A low, guttural growl rumbles from his chest as he rises, shaking the snow from his massive frame. His lips curl back to reveal long, curved canines, a silent warning to whatever dared trespass into his domain. His senses sharpen, the adrenaline coursing through him like wildfire.

He steps out of his den, every muscle taut, as he scans the forest for the source of the disturbance. The scent hits him first: a pack of wolves. They've wandered into his territory, likely unaware they are walking into the realm of the apex predator. He spots them—a group of seven, their lean bodies silhouetted against the silver sheen of the snow. The wolves, emboldened by their numbers, hesitate only briefly when they see him, their eyes narrowing as they consider their options. The tiger lowers his head, his shoulders rolling forward, preparing for what he knows is inevitable.

With a roar that echoes through the forest like thunder, he charges. The wolves scatter, their instincts overriding their arrogance, but their retreat is not without resistance. A few attempt to flank him, snapping at his legs and tail, but their efforts are futile against the tiger's raw power and speed. He lunges at the nearest wolf, his massive paws pinning it to the ground as his jaws clamp down with bone-crushing force. The wolf yelps once before going silent. The pack, realizing the gravity of their mistake, flees into the night, their tails tucked between their legs.

The tiger chases for a few paces, his heart pounding with the thrill of dominance, but he halts as the wolves disappear into the darkness. He knows they can outlast him in a chase—wolves are endurance hunters, built for the long haul, while his own power lies in short, explosive bursts. Satisfied that his message has been received, he turns and begins the trek back to his den. His body aches, his muscles sore from the sudden exertion, but his spirit is unshaken. As he lies down, his eyes close once more, but they remain vigilant, always ready for action. In the tiger's world, survival is not just a matter of strength—it is a constant state of awareness, an unrelenting battle for supremacy in a land of endless challenges.

CHAPTER 7:
TIGERS IN DANGER

Throughout history, humans have waged a tragic campaign against tigers, placing them among the most endangered species on Earth. Nowhere was this brutality more pronounced than during the colonial era in India, where tiger hunting became both a sport and a symbol of dominance. During the British Raj, hunters—often British officials and maharajas—relied on elephants to carry them into the dense jungles. Armed with rifles, they killed indiscriminately. Historical records reveal that by the early 20th century, tens of thousands of tigers were slaughtered in India alone.

The Amur tiger, often referred to as the Siberian tiger, faced its own set of devastating challenges. Once abundant across the Russian Far East, their numbers dwindled dramatically in the 20th century due to hunting for their pelts and body parts, which were highly valued in traditional Chinese medicine. By the 1940s, the Siberian tiger population dropped to fewer than 40 individuals. Today, conservation efforts have brought their numbers to around 500, but they remain at risk due to poaching and habitat encroachment. Tigers in other parts of Asia, such as the South China tiger, experienced an even grimmer fate. The South China tiger has not been seen in the wild since the

1980s and is considered "functionally extinct." Only a handful survive in captivity.

 In the beginning of the 20th century, the world knew nine subspecies of tigers, roaming vast landscapes across Asia. Today, only six subspecies remain, with three tragically extinct in the past century. The Caspian tiger, a magnificent predator native to the forests and river basins of Central Asia, was declared extinct by the 1970s. Hunted relentlessly for sport and to clear land for agriculture, it disappeared after losing over 93% of its habitat. The Javan tiger, another casualty, met its end in the 1980s due to deforestation and overhunting on the island of Java. The Bali tiger, the smallest among its peers, was hunted to extinction by the mid-1940s, never to return to the dense forests of Bali.

 Adding to this tragic list is the critically endangered South China tiger, often considered "functionally extinct." Once abundant in the Chinese wilderness, this tiger has not been observed in the wild for over 35 years. Some experts claim that small, hidden populations might still exist, but most agree that its extinction in the wild is nearly certain. This subspecies fell victim to government-sanctioned eradication campaigns during the mid-20th century, aiming to protect livestock, alongside large-scale deforestation and poaching. Today, any surviving individuals exist only in captivity, with interbreeding among limited populations creating genetic challenges.

The consumption of tiger meat represents a deeply ingrained practice in certain parts of Asia, driven by myths, traditions, and an insatiable demand for the supposed power of the tiger. In countries such as China, Vietnam, and parts of Southeast Asia, the tiger is not only a symbol of strength but also an ingredient in what is considered a luxury experience. Some believe that eating tiger meat, particularly the heart, liver, or bones, transfers the tiger's ferocity, vitality, and courage to the consumer. This belief fuels an illicit but lucrative industry, with black market networks smuggling tiger parts to meet the demands of elite consumers willing to pay exorbitant sums. In some regions, restaurants discreetly offer dishes featuring tiger meat, catering to a wealthy clientele that values the meal as a status symbol as much as a culinary experience.

The industry goes beyond meat consumption.

Tiger bones are often boiled down into tiger bone wine, a product marketed as a remedy for ailments such as arthritis and as a general health tonic. Although banned internationally under the Convention on International Trade in Endangered Species (CITES), such products persist, fueled by centuries-old beliefs and lax enforcement. The farming of tigers for commercial purposes has also exacerbated the problem. In China alone, tiger farms house hundreds of tigers, ostensibly for conservation but, in reality, to cater to the demand for tiger parts. This practice undermines efforts to protect wild populations, as poaching continues to be a cheaper and more direct method of obtaining tigers. Experts estimate that this demand for tiger-derived products is one of the primary threats to their survival, placing immense pressure on already dwindling populations in the wild.

In China, a nation of nearly 1.5 billion people, the estimated number of wild tigers has tragically dwindled to as few as 20. This staggering disparity highlights a heartbreaking reality: a once-thriving apex predator has been reduced to a near-mythical status within its native habitat. Despite efforts to conserve these majestic animals, their numbers have plummeted due to habitat destruction, poaching, and the relentless demand for tiger products. In 2002, a zoo in Thailand called Sriracha Tiger Zoo transferred 100 tigers to Sanya Love World, a zoo in China. After a year, it was discovered that the zoo's shop was selling medicines made from the bones of these tigers. Additionally, the shop was found to be selling tiger meat for consumption. This incident caused a massive outcry in China and around the world, drawing widespread condemnation. The fact that a zoo, intended to be a place of care and preservation for wildlife, was involved in such illegal activities exposed the darker side of the tiger trade. It highlighted how the demand for tiger body parts still fuels the devastating exploitation of these animals, even in settings where they are supposedly protected.

The black market for tiger-derived products is far larger and more organized than most realize. Beyond meat and pelts, tiger bones are crafted into wines, teeth are turned into jewelry, and organs are touted as cures for various ailments. Myths persist, claiming that tiger milk can heal eye problems or that consuming tiger meat imparts the predator's strength and greatness. These baseless beliefs continue to fuel a multi-million-dollar industry, driven by both superstition and greed. To witness such a magnificent animal—engineered by nature to dominate ecosystems—reduced to a commodity for consumption is profoundly disheartening. An apex predator that commands respect and reverence is hunted not out of necessity, but for misguided traditions that science and reason have repeatedly debunked.

The story of Mohan, the first white tiger known to modern history, is a tale of both wonder and tragedy. Discovered in 1951 in the jungles of Rewa, India, Mohan was a rare genetic anomaly, exhibiting a recessive gene that caused his fur to be pure white and his eyes a striking blue. Such occurrences are incredibly rare in nature, estimated to happen in only 1 in 10,000 tiger births. When hunters and locals saw this extraordinary tiger cub, they immediately hunted down his family, killing all of them, and took Mohan alive as a prized specimen. His uniqueness became his curse, setting off a chain of events that would forever alter the genetic future of white tigers.

Today, every white tiger you see in zoos, circuses, or viral social media clips can trace its lineage back to Mohan. This singular lineage is a disaster from a genetic perspective, as it means all white tigers are closely related. Over decades, extensive inbreeding was conducted to preserve the white coat, resulting in severe genetic problems. Studies estimate that up to 80% of white tiger cubs die shortly after birth due to these issues. Those that survive often suffer from deformities, crossed eyes (even in individuals with seemingly normal vision), cleft palates, scoliosis, and weakened immune systems. Despite these ethical concerns, the allure of the white tiger's rarity and beauty keeps breeding programs active, as zoos and private collectors capitalize on their aesthetic appeal.

This obsession with white tigers represents a profound misunderstanding of conservation. These animals, bred for profit and spectacle, often live short, painful lives, and their inbreeding has no role in preserving tiger populations in the wild. Instead of focusing resources on protecting genetically diverse wild tigers, the attention is diverted to a fabricated rarity. The legacy of Mohan, therefore, is bittersweet—a testament to nature's occasional wonders and humanity's recurring hubris in exploiting them.

When India gained its independence in 1947, there was hope that the era of colonial exploitation, including the ruthless hunting of tigers, would come to an end. Under British rule, tiger hunting was a symbol of power and prestige, a sport pursued by royalty and colonial officers alike. During the colonial period, it is estimated that tens of thousands of tigers were killed, reducing the population drastically. With independence, however, the exploitation took a grim new turn. Instead of protecting the tiger, Indian society inadvertently continued the legacy of destruction under the guise of emulating colonial elites.

As British hunters departed, many Indians sought to replicate the sports of the rich as a way of asserting their newfound identity and status. Hunting, once reserved for the elite, became a widespread activity, crossing economic classes. Wealthy landowners, middle-class enthusiasts, and even poorer individuals all aspired to the glamour associated with tiger hunting. Tigers were killed not for survival but for vanity, sportsmanship, and profit. The slaughter escalated, fueled by a black market for tiger pelts, bones, and other parts, which were sold domestically and internationally. By 1970, tiger numbers had plummeted to just 2,500 individuals, a shocking drop from the estimated 50,000 tigers at the turn of the 20th century. This means that 95% of the tiger population was wiped out in less than a century, with many dying brutally for coats, decorations, or unfounded beliefs in medicinal properties.

The devastation marked one of the darkest chapters in the tiger's history. It became evident that the tiger's survival was inextricably linked to cultural shifts and human attitudes. Despite government efforts in later decades to protect the species, the early years of independence proved catastrophic for the Bengal tiger and other subspecies in India. The pursuit of status, wealth, and a misguided sense of power through hunting nearly erased one of the world's most iconic apex predators from the wild.

Throughout history, the tiger population has experienced a dramatic and shocking decline. Once numbering in the tens of thousands, the tiger's presence in the wild has significantly diminished, primarily due to human activities such as poaching, habitat destruction, and illegal wildlife trade. While humans are undoubtedly the main culprits behind this tragic decline, it is also true that, ironically, humans have played a role in the tiger's survival. Efforts to protect tigers, establish reserves, and enforce stricter laws have prevented the complete extinction of these majestic animals. Finally, after decades of relentless exploitation, we are beginning to recognize the importance of preserving nature, not just for our benefit but for the survival of species like the tiger.

Despite this progress, the numbers remain stark. Currently, there are roughly 13,000 tigers globally, a number that includes both those in captivity and those living in the wild. However, the numbers are not as reassuring when you consider that only about 5,000 tigers are left in the wild, while around 8,000 are held in captivity. This means there are more tigers living in captivity than roaming freely in their natural habitats. It's a bitter irony that the very species that commands respect for its strength and beauty is often confined to cages or controlled environments. However, there is a glimmer of hope. As awareness grows and conservation efforts intensify, there is a real possibility that the numbers of wild tigers will increase in the coming years.

We can only hope that by the time you read this book, the number of tigers in the wild has risen significantly, and more tigers are living freely in their natural habitats. The ongoing work to protect and restore tiger populations is critical. While the journey to true recovery is long and fraught with challenges, it is encouraging to see a shift in human attitudes toward wildlife conservation. In the future, we hope to witness the return of more tigers to the wild, as they reclaim their place at the top of the food chain, where they belong.

CHAPTER 8: LEGENDS AND ART

Through history, the tiger has held a unique position, revered in some cultures and misunderstood in others. Its powerful presence in mythology, religion, and literature reflects humanity's complex relationship with this majestic creature. In Taoism, the tiger is not merely an animal but a symbol of cosmic balance. Representing yin energy, it complements the dragon's yang, creating a harmonious balance. Taoist traditions, especially in Taiwan, venerate the Tiger God as a protector against evil spirits and bringer of good fortune. Temples dedicated to this deity depict the tiger as a fierce guardian, its image often carved into gates or altars to ward off misfortune. Rituals involve offerings, prayers, and symbolic acts that reinforce the tiger's role as a sacred entity ensuring harmony in the physical and spiritual realms.

The tiger's significance extends to the Chinese zodiac, where it occupies the third position among the 12 animals. Those born in the Year of the Tiger are believed to embody courage, independence, and competitiveness. The zodiac portrays the tiger as a natural leader, a figure of power and determination. These qualities are celebrated every 12 years during the tiger's cycle, with the last Year of the Tiger in 2022 and the next in 2034. This cycle reflects the tiger's enduring importance in Chinese culture, where its traits are aspired to and admired. The animal's association with protection and bravery can also be seen in Chinese folklore, where stories often depict tigers as guardians of the weak and as adversaries to evil forces threatening the natural order. That means, if you were born in the years 2010, 1998, 1986, 1974, 1962, 1950, or 1938 you were born under the Year of the Tiger.

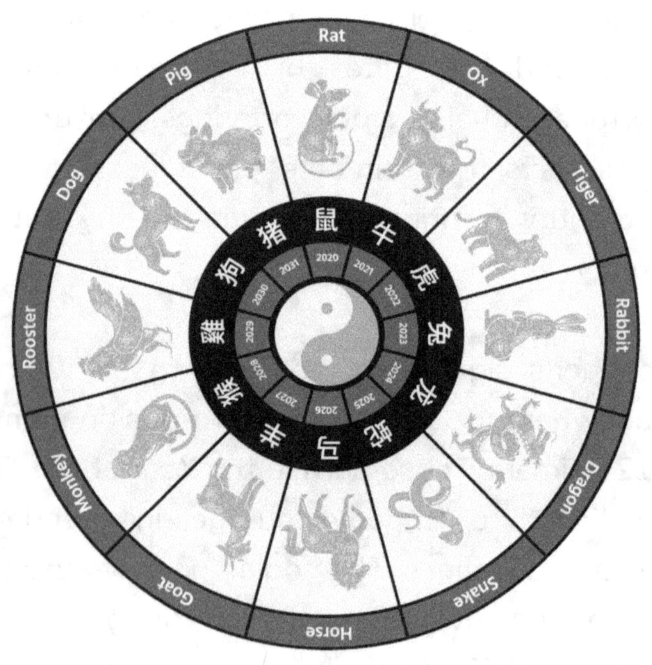

In India, the tiger holds a position of unparalleled reverence and symbolism. Ancient Indian texts frequently depict the tiger as a creature of immense strength and ferocity. In Hindu mythology, the goddess Durga rides a tiger as her mount, symbolizing her dominance over nature and her role as a protector against chaos. The tiger also appears in Buddhist and Jain traditions, where it represents aspects of discipline and the untamed forces of the mind. Beyond mythology, the tiger has been a part of India's royal imagery, adorning banners, coins, and seals of ancient empires such as the Cholas. It was seen as a protector of the realm, a guardian of the jungle, and an emblem of authority. Even today, it is celebrated as the national animal of India, symbolizing the country's rich natural heritage and efforts in wildlife conservation.

Some indigenous tribes in India view the tiger as a spiritual entity and maintain rituals to live in harmony with it. Groups like the Baiga and Gond tribes offer food and prayers to the tiger, believing that such acts protect them from the tiger's predatory instincts. This relationship is a testament to the deep respect and fear that the tiger commands in traditional Indian society. These practices highlight the tiger's role as both a revered and feared being, embodying the delicate balance between coexistence and survival.

In contrast to the Eastern reverence for tigers, Western perspectives have often cast the tiger in a darker light. European literature and art have frequently portrayed the tiger as a symbol of savagery and danger. William Blake's poem The Tyger captures this duality, describing the creature as both a masterpiece of divine creation and a fearful entity. The poem marvels at the tiger's symmetry and beauty while questioning the nature of the power that created it. Similarly, in Rudyard Kipling's The Jungle Book, Shere Khan is depicted as a malevolent antagonist, embodying human fears of the wild and untamed. These portrayals often overshadowed the tiger's role as a guardian of nature, reinforcing its image as a predator rather than a protector.

Western literature contributed to the symbolic "killing" of the tiger in a metaphorical sense. Stories and textbooks studied in Indian schools during colonial times often portrayed the tiger as an adversary of humanity, perpetuating narratives that undermined its cultural significance as a guardian of the jungle. These ideas, coupled with hunting practices during the colonial era, contributed to the physical and ideological decimation of tiger populations. The tiger, once a symbol of pride and strength, was reduced to a villain in the eyes of many.

Jim Corbett's Man-Eaters of Kumaon was published in 1944 and has become a classic in wildlife literature. The book recounts Corbett's experiences hunting man-eating tigers and leopards in India, with one of the tigers, the Champawat Tiger, reportedly responsible for over 400 deaths. This tiger terrorized villages in Nepal and India before Corbett eventually killed it. The book not only gained widespread popularity but has also been studied in some Indian schools, where students examine the shift in perception of the tiger from a noble protector of the jungle to a feared serial killer.

It is true that in Western culture, the tiger was often seen as a symbol of evil, but it was not only viewed through this lens. In addition to the fear and destruction associated with the tiger, there was also a profound admiration for its beauty and strength. While Western influence did contribute to the tragic killing of tigers, this does not mean that all in the West hated them; instead, they were fascinated by the tiger's majesty. One of the most iconic examples of this is the famous poem by William Blake, The Tyger, where he writes:

"Tyger Tyger, burning bright,
In the forests of the night;
What immortal hand or eye,
Could frame thy fearful symmetry?"

In these lines, Blake is not only depicting the tiger as a creature of awe and wonder but also questioning the divine power behind such a perfect yet terrifying being. This complexity of admiration and fear exemplifies the contradictory views of the tiger in the West. The poem is not recent; it was written in 1794.

Today, however, the narrative has shifted. Western countries, once contributors to the tiger's decline, now stand united in efforts to save this magnificent creature from extinction. There are numerous global conservation efforts, with organizations and governments working together to protect tigers and their habitats. The appreciation of the tiger's beauty and strength has evolved into a broader recognition of the need to preserve and protect it for future generations.

Cave art, one of humanity's oldest forms of creative expression, often featured depictions of animals, reflecting the crucial role they played in early human life. Among these animals, large predators like tigers occasionally appeared, symbolizing both reverence and fear. For instance, in regions like the Indian subcontinent and parts of Asia where tigers roamed, early humans created drawings on cave walls to capture their essence. These artworks, often etched or painted using natural pigments, serve as some of the earliest attempts to document interactions with the natural world. The depictions of tigers and similar creatures often emphasize their power and majesty, suggesting that humans regarded them as symbols of strength and danger. While less frequent than other animals such as bison or deer in European caves, tiger-like figures can be interpreted from certain motifs in sites across Asia, indicating their profound significance in prehistoric art.

Over time, the artistic representation of tigers evolved beyond cave walls into more refined mediums, particularly in ancient civilizations like India and China. Sculptures, pottery, and textiles began to feature tiger motifs, often infused with spiritual or mythical meanings. In Indian art, tigers were commonly depicted as guardians, symbolizing protection and valor, and were closely associated with deities like Durga. In Chinese art, tigers represented authority and were often used in architectural designs to signify power and protection. These intricate artworks, whether carved in stone or painted on silk, reflect a deep cultural connection to the tiger, showcasing its role as a bridge between the natural and spiritual worlds.

The reverence for tigers also extended to their symbolic presence in religious and ceremonial art. Beyond physical depictions, these animals became integral to mythologies and rituals, embodying the wild, untamed spirit of nature. Such art forms not only celebrated the tiger's physical prowess but also its spiritual resonance, embedding its image into the cultural fabric of societies that lived alongside it. These artistic endeavors, spanning millennia, ensure that the tiger's legacy endures, offering a glimpse into the profound ways early humans connected with the animal kingdom.

The art of the tiger continues today, especially in Chinese martial arts and popular culture, where the tiger's image is deeply ingrained. It is often used to symbolize strength, ferocity, and precision. In martial arts films or shows, it's not uncommon to hear characters invoking the spirit of the tiger with phrases like "Tiger Strike!" or "Fist of the Tiger!" before executing powerful moves. These moments reflect the tiger's revered status in Chinese folklore and its connection to martial disciplines, where its traits inspire fighting techniques and philosophies. This cultural portrayal keeps the tiger's legacy alive in modern storytelling, blending traditional values with entertainment. The tiger's continued presence in both martial arts and popular media illustrates how deeply it is woven into the fabric of Chinese culture, carrying its powerful symbolism into the present day.

As we can see, tiger culture and its representation in art and traditions have been present for thousands of years, and hopefully, it will continue to be a powerful symbol for millennia to come. It is fascinating to observe how each country and continent has developed its own perception of this magnificent predator. From ancient cave paintings to modern films, the tiger has inspired awe, fear, and admiration, revealing the diverse ways in which humans have related to this majestic creature. Each cultural interpretation adds to the rich tapestry of the tiger's legacy, ensuring its enduring presence in human history and imagination.

Conclusion

In 1872, Charles Darwin delved into the concept of anthropomorphism in his book The Expression of the Emotions in Man and Animals. Darwin argued that humans have a natural tendency to label animals with qualities like good, evil, beauty, or ugliness. This inclination stems from our need to make sense of nature on human terms, projecting our emotions onto creatures that cannot argue back. Such labeling often reflects more about human psychology than the animals themselves.

This leads us to the tiger, a creature often perceived through the lens of anthropomorphism. In truth, the tiger is neither good nor evil—it is simply a predator. Its aggression is a biological necessity for survival, while its aesthetic appeal is a result of natural evolution. This duality of power and beauty has fascinated humanity for centuries, shaping how we see and interact with the tiger.

This combination of beauty and strength, captivating as it may be, does not imbue the tiger with any supernatural powers or mystical healing abilities. The tiger does not possess the means to cure ailments or confer strength upon those who consume parts of its body. Such beliefs, though deeply rooted in certain cultures, stem from human imagination rather than reality. If we take a deeper look at the tiger, we see an animal, neither divine nor superior, striving to survive within the unforgiving natural world. The tiger does not claim greatness, does not demand reverence, and does not elevate itself above humans. It is simply a creature responding to its instincts, navigating its environment, and maintaining its place in the intricate balance of nature.

 And we need to understand that any disruption to the natural cycle, no matter how small, can ripple into far-reaching consequences for ecosystems and humanity alike. The tiger, as a keystone species, plays a critical role in maintaining the delicate balance of its habitat. Removing or significantly reducing its presence could lead to overpopulation of prey species, which in turn might devastate vegetation and disrupt the entire food web. Even changes that seem unrelated to the tiger—such as deforestation, climate shifts, or poaching of smaller animals—can cascade into larger disasters, highlighting how interconnected every element of nature truly is.

 Small changes, whether in the predator population, prey availability, or habitat quality, can spiral into monumental effects. The loss of a single species can trigger a chain reaction, destabilizing entire ecosystems. Recognizing this intricate balance is crucial for humanity, as our own survival is deeply intertwined with the natural world. Every organism, from the tiger to the tiniest insect, contributes to the larger tapestry of life, and our actions today will dictate whether that tapestry remains intact for future generations.

The tiger's future lies in our hands, and with sustained efforts, its habitat can once again flourish with its powerful presence. Let us work toward a world where tigers thrive as a symbol of strength and balance, securing their rightful place in the natural order for generations to come.

References

Books:

"The Tiger: A True Story of Vengeance and Survival" by John Vaillant Alfred, A. Knopf, 2010.
- An enthralling account of a Siberian tiger in the Russian Far East and its interactions with the human world. This book dives into tiger biology, behavior, and conservation challenges.

"Tigers Forever: Saving the World's Most Endangered Big Cat" by Steve Winter and Sharon Guynup, National Geographic, 2013.
- A blend of stunning photography and insightful writing that discusses the threats to tiger survival and efforts to protect them.

"Tigers in Red Weather" by Ruth Padel, Walker Books, 2005.
- This book offers a poetic and deeply personal journey into the lives of tigers, covering their natural history, mythology, and modern conservation struggles.

Documentaries:

-"The Tiger Next Door" (Full Documentary).
-David Attenborough's Tigers: Spy in the Jungle.
-Da77e7 Youtube Episode: "Tiger" by New Media Academy Life.

The Next Book
"THE LION: KING OF THE SAVANNAH"

The next chapter of Big Cats: Nature's Perfection takes us from the dense jungles to the open plains of Africa, where the lion holds dominion as the ultimate predator. Revered as a symbol of power and royalty, the lion's social dynamics, hunting prowess, and cultural significance are unparalleled. In "The Lion: King of the Savannah", we will explore the myths, stories, and realities surrounding this magnificent creature, offering insights into its survival challenges and timeless legacy. Prepare to be captivated by the king of beasts in this thrilling continuation of the series.

www.ingramcontent.com/pod-product-compliance
Lightning Source LLC
Chambersburg PA
CBHW050825250726

48653CB00006B/2423